W.
Ol
NORTH YORK MOORS

Book two – Southern moors
Rosedale, Farndale and the Tabular Hills

HILLSIDE GUIDES

LONG DISTANCE WALKS

CIRCULAR WALKS IN THE YORKSHIRE DALES

CIRCULAR WALKS ON THE NORTH YORK MOORS

WALKS
ON THE
NORTH YORK MOORS
BOOK TWO – SOUTHERN
Rosedale, Farndale and the Tabular Hills

by

Paul Hannon

HILLSIDE PUBLICATIONS

HILLSIDE PUBLICATIONS
11 Nessfield Grove
Exley Head
Keighley
West Yorkshire
BD22 6NU

Cover illustration: on Bridestones Moor
Page 1: Hutton – le – Hole

ISBN   1 870141 05 9

Printed in Great Britain by
Carnmor Print and Design
95/97 London Road
Preston
Lancashire
PR1 4BA

INTRODUCTION

THE NORTH YORK MOORS NATIONAL PARK

The North York Moors is the fourth largest of our ten National Parks, designated in 1952 with an area of 553 square miles. It is probably the best-defined upland area of all, rising island-like from the surrounding countryside. This creates an impression of much greater altitude than its very modest summit of 1490 feet attains. If asked which of the Parks is bottom of the height table, few would be likely to provide the correct answer, the North York Moors.

To the north is the Cleveland Plain, westwards the Vales of Mowbray and York, and southwards the Vale of Pickering while to the east is the ultimate low point, the North Sea. The Park itself however has a solid upland mass spreading from the centre towards the western escarpments, where one can walk for mile upon mile and lose little altitude. It is of course all this heather-clad moorland for which the National Park is best known, for there is no similar expanse anywhere else in the country.

Heather moors, despite their profusion, are only one aspect of this diverse region, for here are some delightful green valleys and a spectacular length of coastline composed largely of rugged cliffs. There are sandy shorelines and rocky coves, and inland some shapely summits, fascinating rock outcrops, beautiful waterfalls, and despite all the forestry some enchanting indigenous woods remain. The hand of man has been everywhere, even on the lonely moortops which are littered with ancient burial mounds and standing stones. The scores of villages range from fishing ports to moorland farming communities, though many of the villages are to be found beneath the hills, taking advantage of their shelter.

Man has also left ruined abbeys and castles; some old roads including a drovers' route, a Roman road and numerous paved trods; absorbing relics of the former ironstone, alum and jet industries; and not least of all an unrivalled collection of wayside crosses, some being ancient Christian symbols, and others serving as waymarks or boundary stones.

This is walkers territory par excellence, with a plethora of long-distance and challenge walks crossing it. Best known are the first, the poor old Lyke Wake Walk, and the longest and best, the Cleveland Way.

The three titles in this series of guides cover the whole of the National Park, and are divided into three necessarily arbitrary but nevertheless well-defined areas.

5

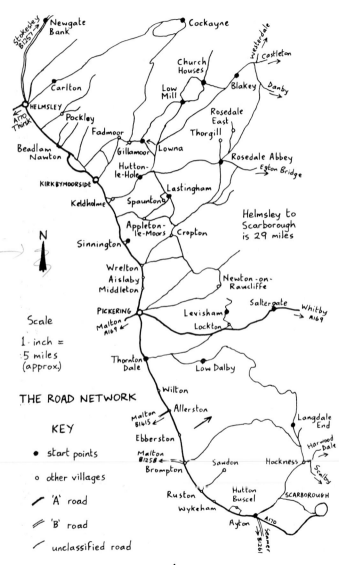

THE ROAD NETWORK

KEY

- • start points
- ○ other villages
- ⟋ 'A' road
- ⟍ 'B' road
- ⟋ unclassified road

Scale

1 inch =
5 miles
(approx.)

Helmsley to
Scarborough
is 29 miles

N

THE SOUTHERN MOORS

The subject of this volume is the southern area of the Park, which takes the form of a string of parallel but highly individual valleys running south from the high moors at the heart of the district. Further east the moors give way to softer environs, eventually becoming suffocated by the extensive forests. The valleys include, from west to east, Bransdale, Farndale, Rosedale, Newton Dale, Thornton Dale and the Derwent valley.

As the rivers and becks run off the moors, they encounter the other dominating feature of the area, namely the Tabular Hills. These crouching lions are ranged along the entire length of the southern moors, rising almost imperceptibly from the Vale of Pickering to then plunge sharply at their northern limit. Their table-top appearance - hence the name- means that one needs to be in the right place to appreciate their sleek profiles: this is usually either on the same latitude or to their north. Fortunately this is where most of the walks will be found.

The highest and shapeliest of these hills occupy the western half of the area, where the major dales narrow in order to break through into the flat vale. These Tabular Hills provide shelter for most of the villages in the district, though some are bravely perched on the plateau-like tops. A regular feature of these communities is the long, wide main street, often with little other development, while some of the dale villages are graced with attractive becks flowing through their very centres: some are huge tourist draws, others retain their solitude.

USING THIS GUIDE

Described in this book are 18 walks ranging in length from 4 to 8 miles. With an average distance of 5½ miles, they are ideally suited to half-day rambles. All are circular and begin from either a car park or a sensible parking location. Each of the walks has its own chapter, made easy to find by its number at the top corner of the page. Each chapter comprises of an 'immediate impression' diagram, detailed narrative and strip-map, and notes and illustrations of features of interest.

Although the strip-maps illustrating each walk should guide one safely around, they show nothing of the surrounding countryside, and for this purpose an Ordnance Survey map is to be recommended. The 1-inch Tourist map covers the entire Park, and is therefore the perfect companion. It also serves to locate the start-points with ease. Pages 10 and 11 list each walk, length and start-point, along with an outline location map.

SOME USEFUL FACILITIES

	Accommodation	Inn	Car park	Bus service	Post Office	other shop	Payphone	WC
Appleton-le-Moors	✓	✓		✓	✓		✓	
Ayton	✓	✓		✓	✓	✓	✓	
Blakey	✓	✓	✓	✓				
Church Houses	✓	✓					✓	
East Moors							✓	
Gillamoor	✓	✓			✓		✓	
Hutton-le-Hole	✓	✓	✓	✓	✓	✓	✓	✓
Langdale End		✓		✓			✓	
Lastingham	✓	✓		✓	✓		✓	
Levisham	✓	✓			✓		✓	
Low Dalby			✓				✓	✓
Low Mill	✓		✓		✓		✓	✓
Lowna			✓					
Newgate Bank			✓	✓				
Rosedale Abbey	✓	✓	✓	✓	✓	✓	✓	✓
Rosedale East	✓				✓		✓	
Saltergate			✓	✓	✓			
Sinnington	✓	✓		✓	✓		✓	
Staindale			✓					✓
Thornton Dale	✓	✓	✓	✓	✓	✓	✓	✓

All known details are listed for the places visited on the walks. There are also youth hostels at Helmsley, Lockton and Scarborough. The trio of small market towns to the south, Helmsley, Kirkbymoorside and Pickering, provide all services along with Scarborough which also has a rail service.

This is a general guide only.

SOME USEFUL ADDRESSES

Ramblers' Association
  1/5 Wandsworth Road, London SW8 2LJ
    Tel. 01-582 6878

Youth Hostels Association
  Trevelyan House, St. Albans, Herts. AL1 2DY
    Tel. St. Albans (0727) 55215

North York Moors National Park
    Information Service
  The Old Vicarage, Bondgate, Helmsley, York
    Tel. Helmsley (0439) 70657

The Moors Centre (National Park Visitor Centre)
  Danby, Whitby, North Yorkshire YO21 2NB
    Tel. Castleton (0287) 60654

Pickering Station Information Centre
  Pickering, North Yorkshire YO18 7AJ
    Tel. Pickering (0751) 73791

Ryedale Folk Museum Information Centre
  Hutton-le-Hole, York YO6 6UA
    Tel. Lastingham (07515) 367

Yorkshire and Humberside Tourist Board
  312 Tadcaster Road, York YO2 2HF
    Tel. York (0904) 707961

Forestry Commission
  42 Eastgate, Pickering, N. Yorks. YO18 7DU
    Tel. Pickering (0751) 72771

The National Trust - Regional Office
  Goddards, 27 Tadcaster Rd, York YO2 2QG
    Tel. York (0904) 702021

Scarborough and District Bus Company
  Valley Bridge Bus Station, Scarborough
    Tel. Scarborough (0723) 375463

THE WALKS

Listed below are the 18 walks described, the walk number being the key to easy location in the guide

THE WALKS

- 1 Sinnington
- 2 Saltergate
- 3 Low Dalby
- 4 Rosedale Abbey
- 5 Lowna
- 6 Thornton Dale
- 7 Carlton
- 8 Ayton
- 9 Levisham
- 10 Low Mill
- 11 Church Houses
- 12 Lastingham
- 13 Newgate Bank
- 14 Blakey
- 15 Saltergate
- 16 Langdale End
- 17 Cockayne
- 18 Hutton-le-Hole

Outline map of routes and starting points

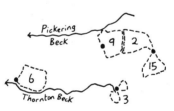

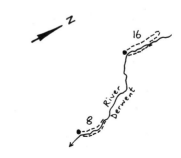

11

WALK 1

5 miles

APPLETON-LE-MOORS AND THE SEVEN

from Sinnington

Two neighbouring
villages are
linked by
pleasant routes
involving fine
riverside
woodland
paths

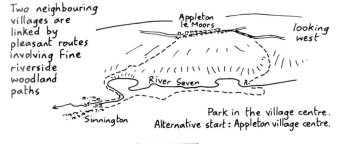

Park in the village centre.
Alternative start: Appleton village centre.

THE WALK

Leave the village by the road heading up the east side of the river above the bridge by the green. Passing a fork to the church, the road becomes a track at the last house and drops down to the river. When the Seven loops away the track continues along the bottom of the wood, soon rising a little to a crossroads in the trees on a tiny ridge. Here turn up to the right but very soon leave the track on a bend and continue straight along a narrow path. Levelling out, it leaves the trees at a stile and runs along the top of a row of trees to another stile into a wood. An excellent path now runs above the river before dropping down to its bank.

When the Seven loops away again we continue once more along the bottom of the wood. At a fork take the rising path to another crossroads on a small ridge, and cross straight over to a track descending the other side. The wood is left along a short enclosed way, at the end of which resist the slope in front but turn left to the near-again riverbank. This is followed downstream to be forded at the weir at Appleton Mill Farm (easy in normal conditions). Turn right in front of the buildings and out along the access road, which turns left to climb up to join a narrow lane. Continue straight up to a T-junction at the top of Appleton-le-Moors village.

Turn left to take in the entire length of this broad main street, and at the sharp bend at the far end keep straight on down a short farm track into a field. Head down this and the following field-edges as far as a gate causing a

12

tiny kink in the accompanying hedge. Here the field track ends and through the gate we cross the field to a gate into a wood. A good path then resumes high above the river to a gate back out of the trees. From here a wide track clings to the tree-lined Seven to lead back into Sinnington, with the bridge returning us to the main part of the village on the east bank.

Low Cross

Appleton-le-Moors

Main Street

Appleton-le-Moors is a classically laid out village with a broad main street, our traverse of which is likely to induce the theme tune of *High Noon*. Parallel back lanes run along the rear of both rows of gradely dwellings. The distinguished church dates from 1865, and a Wesleyan chapel from 1832. Look out for the house of three faces.

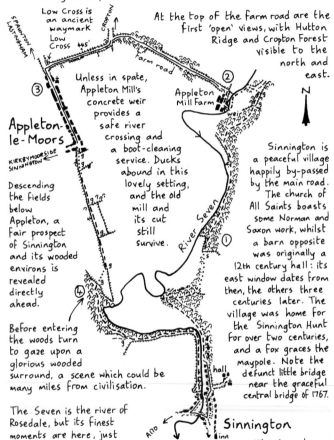

Low Cross is an ancient waymark Low Cross 445'

At the top of the farm road are the first 'open' views, with Hutton Ridge and Cropton Forest visible to the north and east.

SPAUNTON LASTINGHAM

CROPTON

Farm road

N

(2)

Appleton Mill Farm

weir

Appleton-le-Moors

(3)

KIRKBYMOORSIDE SINNINGTON ←

Unless in spate, Appleton Mill's concrete weir provides a safe river crossing and a boot-cleaning service. Ducks abound in this lovely setting, and the old mill and its cut still survive.

Descending the fields below Appleton, a fair prospect of Sinnington and its wooded environs is revealed directly ahead.

Before entering the woods turn to gaze upon a glorious wooded surround, a scene which could be many miles from civilisation.

River Seven

(1)

(4)

The Seven is the river of Rosedale, but its finest moments are here, just above Sinnington, where it loops through some exquisite (and popular) wooded environs.

Sinnington is a peaceful village happily by-passed by the main road. The church of All Saints boasts some Norman and Saxon work, whilst a barn opposite was originally a 12th century hall: its east window dates from then, the others three centuries later. The village was home for the Sinnington Hunt for over two centuries, and a fox graces the maypole. Note the defunct little bridge near the graceful central bridge of 1767.

hall

A170

A170

Sinnington

inn

The Seven leaves the National Park at Sinnington.

WALK 2

THE HOLE OF HORCUM

7½ miles

from Saltergate

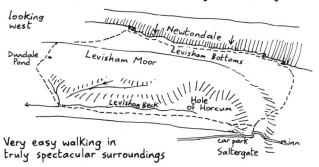

looking west

Dundale Pond

Levisham Moor

Newtondale

Levisham Bottoms

Levisham Beck

Hole of Horcum

car park Saltergate

Inn

Very easy walking in truly spectacular surroundings

Start from the large car-park atop Saltergate Bank on the A169, half a mile south of the inn.

THE WALK

From the car park cross the main road to a path parallel with it, and head north as far as the hairpin bend on Saltergate Bank. Here take the left-hand of two stiles on the left to descend immediately into the Hole of Horcum. The path heads through bracken to a stile and continues on past the derelict Low Horcum. Just beyond, fork right on a narrow trod through a long pasture in the narrowing dale.

On approaching the wood above, fork right to stay outside its fence, soon crossing a couple of stiles to drop down very gradually to a footbridge over the tree-lined Levisham Beck. Crossing this and then the inflowing beck just beyond, a guidepost is reached indicating a path up to the right. A good path indeed rises above Dundale Griff onto the moor top. At a fork, take the narrower right-hand path to arrive at Dundale Pond.

From this Piccadilly Circus of tracks head away in the same direction as before, skirting the left side of the pond to continue straight on to a wall-corner on the left. At this crossroads of paths turn right, over the brow of the moor and down West Side Brow to cross to the prominent Skelton Tower. Now turn right along the top of the steep drop to Newtondale, eventually merging with another path after an old quarry.

A good three-quarter mile's easy walking after the old quarry take a lesser path left to return to the top of the escarpment. A narrow path now runs along the edge, soon with steep cliffs adding to the atmosphere: this is no place for young children to be playing! Eventually a wall bars the way, so go right with it until it turns away. Now continue straight on towards Saltergate Bank, on an improving path which crosses the near-level moor before a steep pull to join a fence. The path then heads away with the fence to a stile, where our outward route is joined near the hairpin bend in the road. Steps can now be retraced up the parallel path back to the car park.

Skelton Tower is a notable landmark standing on the rim of the sudden drop to the floor of Newton Dale. Arrival here is quite a spectacular event. The tower was built as a shooting lodge in the early 19th century by the vicar of Levisham, Robert Skelton. A partial restoration by the National Park authority in 1978 made the ruin safe.

Newton Dale

Skelton Tower

old quarry

Levisham Bottoms

④

The Bottoms is a well-defined level section of moorland between steeper slopes above and below.

this sunken track probably once served the former quarry.

× 694'

× prominent tumulus

The word 'griff' appears regularly in this area but rarely elsewhere. It describes a small steep-sided valley, often dry and with rock outcrops.

Levisham Moor

③

Dundale Pond

this wide track provides a rapid return to the start point if needed.

Dundale Pond is an artificial sheet of water thought to have been the work of monks of Malton Priory in the 13th century, to cater for their flocks and herds which grazed here. This reed-fringed pool stands at a busy little junction of moorland tracks.

Dundale Griff

Levisham Beck

②

16

Despite its cloak of afforestation, Newton Dale still remains a dramatic setting by virtue of the deep groove it has carved through the moors. At its northern limit the valley merges very tamely with that of Eller Beck, which flows north through Goathland and into Eskdale. This natural pass is the most obvious in the entire breadth of the moors, and was consequently exploited by George Stephenson who constructed his Whitby-Pickering railway through here. The line between Grosmont and Pickering was saved by a preservation society and is now one of the National Park's major attractions.

From Skelton Tower to Yewtree Scar we follow (or are close to) the steep drop to the valley, and in season are likely to witness a steam train.

Newton Dale

Huggitt's Scar

Yewtree Scar

⑤

⑥

Yewtree Scar from Huggitt's Scar

The path above Huggitt's Scar is on land in the care of the National Park Authority.

Hole of Horcum

clearly discernable → Cross Dyke

Low Horcum

①

At 920' the start point is also the highest!

Levisham Beck

WHITBY A169

inn

⑦

Salter-gate

see Walk 15

car park

PICKERING A169 →

Skelton Tower

The Hole of Horcum is a famous feature alongside the busy A169. It takes the form of an enormous bowl which nature has carved out of the moors, and to date it remains untamed by the plough.

WALK 3

$3\frac{1}{2}$ miles

STAINDALE AND THE BRIDESTONES

from Low Dalby

Two short
walks are
linked to
create a
worthwhile
exercise.
Bridestones
Moor is a
little gem.

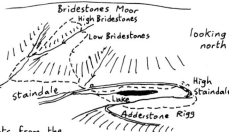

The walk starts from the
Staindale car-parks, 3 miles
north of Low Dalby on the Forest Drive (toll payable) through
Dalby Forest. A toilet block helps confirm the location.

THE WALK

From the car-park below the toilets (on the north
side of the road), take the sketchy path past the picnic
tables to the National Trust sign, beyond which a path leads
to two stiles. Take the right-hand one (and subsequent left
fork) for a steep climb through the trees onto Bridestones Moor.
The climbing ends above the trees, and the path heads straight
across the moor to the Low Bridestones just ahead.

On reaching the stones our path continues on past
them all and down to a beck before rising to the neighbouring
High Bridestones. At the third of these it turns sharp left, but
a short detour right is recommended until the rocks expire.
Back on the main path it now descends a modest ridge to a
plank over a beck, then continues through a long pasture to
a footbridge back over the beck. Just beyond is a stile, and
from it turn left to run along the top of several fields to
return to the other stile at the starting point. The car park
is just a minute or two further.

To extend the walk head up to the toilets then
drop down to the beckside. A vague path heads upstream by
a picnic site beneath the dam of Staindale Lake. Go left
along the dam to the roadside, then follow the shore up to
another car park. At the hairpin bend in the road behind go

along the forest road between the buildings at High Staindale, then right at an early fork. Beyond a gate bear right again, and then leave the track when the right-hand fence does. Go with it and a good path soon materialises to rise through the undergrowth, climbing continually until a wide forest track is met.

Go right along this track until a lesser track forks left, but instead of taking it use a footpath which drops down to the right onto the 'Forest Drive' road. Cross straight over and down a good path to a footbridge over Staindale Beck. A few yards up the slope is the road, and across it is the start point.

Of the several bridestones scattered about the North York Moors, these are the best known. The two groupings of distinctive rocks have been created by natural weather erosion of their Jurassic sandstone, and these weird sculptures are even further enhanced by their setting on the bracken-covered Bridestones Moor. From the stones it will be noticed that the moor is but an island surrounded by forestry (north and east) and farmland (south and west).

The moor is owned by the National Trust and run jointly with the Yorkshire Naturalists' Trust.

Much of this walk makes use of National Trust and Forestry Commission permissive paths.

Low Dalby is a Forestry Commission village with a Forest Visitor Centre which makes a worthwhile stopping point en route to the start of the walk. The Commission's policy is to encourage public usage, from the Forest Drive to innumerable trails. The centre has leaflets and various other publications on sale.

Dalby Forest is a popular stage on motoring rallies, though it is advisable for normal visitors to take the Forest Drive toll road a little more leisurely.

A Bridestones Nature Trail has been established, with an informative leaflet available.

The lake is artificial but nevertheless, with its birdlife, rather pleasant.

WALK 4
5½ miles

THE HEART OF ROSEDALE

from Rosedale Abbey

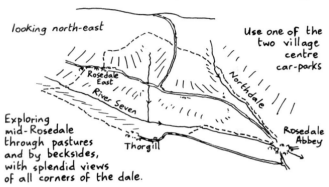

looking north-east

Use one of the two village centre car-parks

Rosedale East

River Seven

Northdale

Rosedale Abbey

Thorgill

Exploring mid-Rosedale through pastures and by becksides, with splendid views of all corners of the dale.

THE WALK

     Leave the village centre at a footpath sign midway between the car park opposite the green, and the toilets just a little further along the road to Castleton. A short enclosed way soon empties into a field, and here we turn left to head upstream with Northdale Beck. The barely discernable path keeps company with the beck through numerous fields, at last rising to a gate after the only ladder-stile encountered. Cross the field to a smaller gate and then return to the beck, using a tiny slab bridge to cross it.

     From the bridge take the sketchy track heading right alongside a wall, continuing on above the trees to join a farm road. Cross straight over to a gate and rise up the field, through a gate and on to the top corner of a fence at the start of a tiny beck. Walk alongside the fence to join a track rising from the barn on the right, to then zig-zag up to a gate onto a road.

     Cross the road to the stile opposite and go right with the fence before dropping gradually to a stile at the far bottom corner. From the gate behind it a path runs along the bottom of a young plantation before a short rise onto a wide green path. Turn left along it until shortly after swinging left after a beck crossing. At an old fence the path forks, and here drop down left through encroaching trees to escape them at a stile. Cross half-right to a gap in a fence and continue on to pass along the front of Clough House. The access track leads away to join a better track, turning left down it to meet the road in Rosedale East.

Turn right along the road as far as the post office, where a footpath sign points down the surfaced road alongside. At the farmyard at the bottom continue straight down the fieldside to a footbridge over the river Seven. Rise up the field behind to a gate onto a track between hedgerows, and turn left along it to eventually meet the road end at Thorgill.

Head through the hamlet and remain on the road for a short half-mile until a stile and footpath sign point the way down a field to a footbridge to re-cross the Seven. Turn right along a path which leaves the trees at a stile to soon rise to a fence corner, then running along the fence-top to another stile. A caravan site appears below, and our path eventually merges with its access track at a wicket-gate. Head along the track past a recreation area until neighbouring signs give a choice of how to re-enter Rosedale Abbey. Turn right along the back road to locate the green.

Rosedale Abbey is a lovely village in the true heart of the National Park. It is also a busy little place, with hostelries, shops and caravan sites all in the plural. Its name stems from the existence of a Cistercian nunnery founded here in the 12th century. What little remains stands forlornly in a small enclosure behind the church, much having been plundered for dwellings during the 19th century iron boom (see also Walk 14). Roads radiate from strategically sited Rosedale Abbey, including two which cross the high moors to a wide range of Eskdale villages.

the church and nunnery ruins

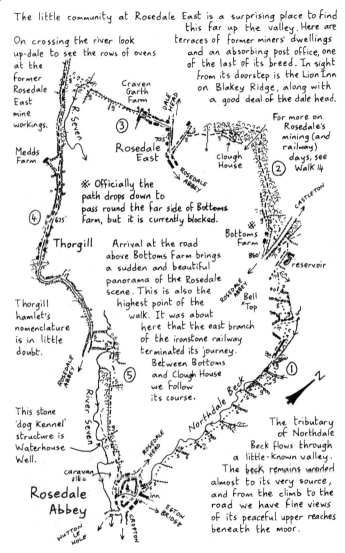

The little community at Rosedale East is a surprising place to find this far up the valley. Here are terraces of former miners' dwellings and an absorbing post office, one of the last of its breed. In sight from its doorstep is the Lion Inn on Blakey Ridge, along with a good deal of the dale head.

On crossing the river look up-dale to see the rows of ovens at the former Rosedale East mine workings.

Craven Garth Farm

Medds Farm

③ Rosedale East

For more on Rosedale's mining (and railway) days, see Walk 14

②

Clough House

CASTLETON

※ Officially the path drops down to pass round the far side of Bottoms Farm, but it is currently blocked.

④ 1625'

Thorgill

Bottoms Farm 860'

reservoir

Arrival at the road above Bottoms Farm brings a sudden and beautiful panorama of the Rosedale scene. This is also the highest point of the walk. It was about here that the east branch of the ironstone railway terminated its journey. Between Bottoms and Clough House we follow its course.

Bell ✕ Top

Thorgill hamlet's nomenclature is in little doubt.

⑤

This stone 'dog kennel' structure is Waterhouse Well.

①

Northdale Beck

caravan

Rosedale Abbey

inn

EGTON BRIDGE

CROPTON

HUTTON LE HOLE

The tributary of Northdale Beck flows through a little-known valley. The beck remains unwooded almost to its very source, and from the climb to the road we have fine views of its peaceful upper reaches beneath the moor.

WALK 5

5¼ miles

from Lowna

looking north-east

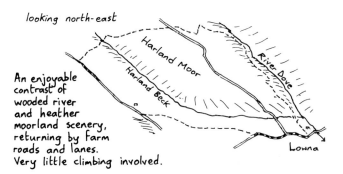

An enjoyable
contrast of
wooded river
and heather
moorland scenery,
returning by farm
roads and lanes.
Very little climbing involved.

Start from the small car-park just west of Lowna farm and bridge on the Gillamoor to Hutton-le-Hole road.

THE WALK

From the car park don't return to the road, but instead take the track leaving the rear of the parking area. It soon narrows to drop down to cross a beck before reaching a guidepost and fork. Take the left one which soon passes an old Quaker burial ground before rising across the bottom of Harland Moor alongside a wall. At a gate take the path down to a junction above the river, and then turn to follow the path upstream. It runs through bracken above the Dove before dropping down to its bank to shortly arrive at a footbridge.

Don't cross the river but take the path climbing steeply left: it soon eases to swing right, and before long a stile by a gate takes us onto the moor. Our track heads towards a forest fence, but a little before reaching it take a track doubling back up to the left. Another fence is soon met, and from the stile there rise the few yards up to a wide track. Go right along it for about 50 yards to locate a narrow but well-defined trod which rises left, past a wall-corner and onto a moorland road.

At a pair of footpath signs cross straight over and along a good landrover track through the heather

23

of Harland Moor. Descending gradually it eventually leaves the moor at a gate, and a few yards further a gate on the left precedes a footbridge over Harland Beck. Take the track away from it up to a wall-corner, crossing a rough pasture to a gate between wall and fence. From it take the narrower right-hand path through the heather, diagonally crossing a curious little moor to a gate onto a road.

Turn left along the road to soon drop down to pass Grays Farm set back on the left. Continue two fields further to the start of a steep climb and then escape left at a bridleway sign and a gate. Drop down to another gate and then sharp right to accompany the right-hand field boundary for a long stretch before briefly entering a wooded area. Just beyond is a fork, the right arm leaving the trees to run between hedgerows to Faddell Rigg Farm, continuing past it onto a road.

Turn left along the road to soon return to the car park just beyond the Farndale junction.

Lowna is nothing more than a farmstead, but the prominent (from the road bridge) large old building was once a tannery. This is a delightful setting by the river Dove, with the steep Gillamoor Bank rising to that village, less than a mile distant. Easily missed near the beginning of the walk is the Quaker burial ground, which takes the form of a small walled enclosure at the bottom corner of a wood. A notice by the gate records the fact that between the years 1675 and 1837, 114 Friends were buried on this site.

Boon Hill
from
Harland Moor

Harland Moor is a fine area of moorland divided by the Gillamoor – Low Mill road. Colourful bracken slopes interspersed with rowan descend almost to the river, and during our climb to the road there are superb views up into the heart of Farndale.

Above the road Harland Moor is a classic heather terrain, with views now to the south of a range of Tabular Hills. Boon Hill, and to its right, Birk Nab, are the most prominent.

COCKAYNE

Hope Inn Farm

Grays (Farm)

Grays farm has the appearance of the Danish-style Long house.

Harland Beck

Harland Moor

summit of walk

695'

LOW MILL

GILLAMOOR

GILLAMOOR

Having escaped the excitement of its daffodil crowds above Low Mill, the river Dove settles down to flow through some exquisitely wooded and peaceful environs. Shunning any further publicity it glides out of the Park to join the Rye in the Vale of Pickering. NB- The daffodils extend much further, but the public paths don't.

Faddell Rigg (Farm)

Quaker burial ground

LOW MILL

car park

GILLAMOOR

Lowna

farm

N

HUTTON-LE-HOLE

River Dove

On crossing Harland Moor one may notice the heather growing in patches of varying height, some of which might be completely bare. This is a result of the common practice known as 'swiddening', when controlled burning of the heather helps generate succulent young shoots for the grouse.

25

WALK 6

6 miles

HOWL DALE AND ELLERBURN

From Thornton Dale

looking north-west

Howl Dale

Ellerburn

Thornton Dale

Fields, woods and lanes combine for a

Use the large village centre car-park.

simple stroll in the hinterland of lovely Thornton Dale.
NB: *This walk is best enjoyed after a dry spell.*

THE WALK

From the village centre take the main road towards Pickering, and leave it at the brow of the hill (care is required crossing from the footpath to the north side of the road) by a signposted footpath at a stile just beyond a lane rising away. Cross to the field corner and maintain the direction across the next field, then cross straight over the next two before clinging to the top of the last field before entering a wood. A path then heads down to a gate to the drive at Hagg House Farm.

Turn left over the cattle-grid and then leave by the first gate on the right. Follow the fence away to a stile into some trees, a path then materialising to swing down to the right to commence the long journey up wooded Howl Dale. The path clings to the floor of this narrow valley for well over a mile, as far as an intervening gate. Here turn up to a stile on the left, to resume the journey on the outside of the trees along the field bottom.

Remain with the fence to the field corner, where a stile will be found pointing unconvincingly into an area of scrub. A vague path heads away to join a better one, turning left to immediately meet a wide track. Turn right up this to soon leave the trees and eventually empty onto a road. Head left to the first junction, then right towards the Dalby Forest drive. At the first bend leave this road also, by a path down through the trees on the right. Part-way it meets a wider path to soon leave the trees, descending a field-edge to emerge alongside the church at Ellerburn.

Turn right up the gated access road to return to Thornton Dale. At a junction turn down the road through a mill yard, the road then running along by the attractive beck. When the beck parts company with the road remain with the former, on a footpath that emerges via a 'chocolate box' scene onto the main road through the village.

Thornton
Dale

Ellerburn Church

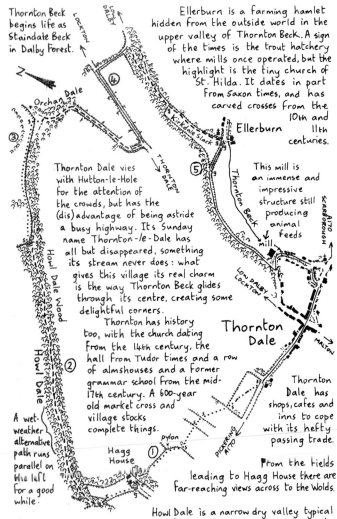

Thornton Beck begins life as Staindale Beck in Dalby Forest.

Ellerburn is a farming hamlet hidden from the outside world in the upper valley of Thornton Beck. A sign of the times is the trout hatchery where mills once operated, but the highlight is the tiny church of St. Hilda. It dates in part from Saxon times, and has carved crosses from the 10th and 11th centuries.

Ellerburn

This mill is an immense and impressive structure still producing animal feeds

mill

Thornton Dale vies with Hutton-le-Hole for the attention of the crowds, but has the (dis)advantage of being astride a busy highway. Its Sunday name Thornton-le-Dale has all but disappeared, something its stream never does: what gives this village its real charm is the way Thornton Beck glides through its centre, creating some delightful corners.

Thornton has history too, with the church dating from the 14th century, the hall from Tudor times and a row of almshouses and a former grammar school from the mid-17th century. A 600-year old market cross and village stocks complete things.

Thornton Dale

Thornton Dale has shops, cafes and inns to cope with its hefty passing trade.

A wet-weather alternative path runs parallel on the left for a good while.

Hagg House

From the fields leading to Hagg House there are far-reaching views across to the Wolds.

Howl Dale is a narrow dry valley typical of many on the southern edge of the moors. Heavily wooded, it displays a good mixture of trees giving splendid autumn colours.

WALK 7

7 miles

BIRK NAB AND EAST MOORS

from Carlton

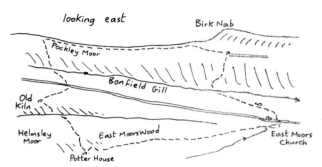

looking east

Pockley Moor · Birk Nab · Bonfield Gill · Old Kiln · Helmsley Moor · East Moors Wood · Potter House · East Moors Church

A highly varied walk in a lesser-known corner of the Moors

Start from the isolated East Moors church, 2½ miles north of Carlton village, on the Bransdale road (4½ miles north of Helmsley). There is verge parking opposite the church.

THE WALK

It is intended that the confusing footpath network in the neighbourhood of the church is to be rationalised at a future date. Any alterations will be clearly signposted.

Take the footpath leaving the road alongside the churchyard wall, through a small gate and straight on to a gate into a field. Follow its left side to the next gate, then straight ahead to the access road to Lund Farm. Go forward on it to the gate in front, and when it turns down to the farm continue on for a steady descent along the right side of several fields to arrive at Bonfield Gill. If swollen its crossing may be a little difficult, but once across a sketchy track rises half-right to a wall, then rising with it to meet the surfaced road-end at Birk Nab Farm.

Without entering the farmyard turn left along a vague track outside the farm wall. At the next gate it then becomes sunken and well-defined, crossing a rough pasture before emerging onto the open moor. Our track heads north across the moor to soon merge with a wider track running along the very broad ridge. This is followed for almost a mile, rising gently all the way to a crossroads of tracks. Here turn left to drop down to a beck (Bonfield Gill again), and having enjoyed an easier crossing, climb the slope until just beyond the wall corner. Here the main track is vacated in favour of a narrower one which rises more steadily to the left to join the open road to Bransdale.

Cross straight over the road and along the farm track opposite, turning left at an early fork to drop down to the buildings of Old Kiln. On entering its confines turn immediately left to another gate, then sharp right to a gate beyond which a wall is followed straight down to Bogmire Gill. On the slope opposite a path rises through the plantation to meet a forest road: head straight up the wide track directly ahead, over the brow to a gate out of the trees.

Follow the left-hand fence away to the first gate, then cross the field to Potter House. Without entering its yard turn back to the left across this same field to a gate into a bracken-filled pasture. Contour right across it on a decent track which fades before gaining the barns that were once Snaper Farm.

Keep to the left of the buildings and accompany the access track away to a gate into the forest. Here turn immediately right inside the forest boundary, then right again with the fence. Only a little further and the track turns left to plunge deep into the trees. Soon the track becomes a mere path, which runs on, however, to join a forest road.

Continue left along it to a merging of three such roads at a gate. Turn down through it to a footbridge and ford, then up to join the Bransdale road again. The church is now just a few yards up to the left.

④

Old Kiln · ruinous kiln

Bogmire Gill

⑤

Helmsley Moor

* footpath unofficially diverted outside the long pasture

East Moors Wood

Potter House (Farm)   barns *

⑥

Birk Nab from the north

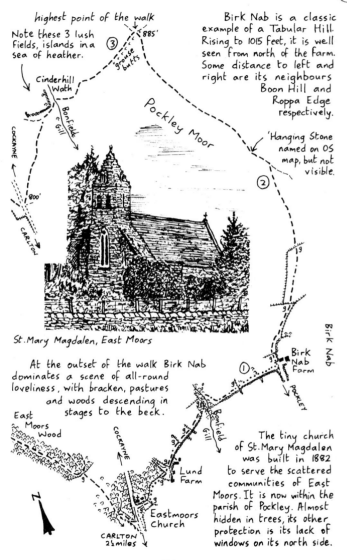

highest point of the walk

Note these 3 lush fields, islands in a sea of heather.

885'

③

grouse butts

Cinderhill Wath

Bonfield Gill

COCKAYNE ←

800'

CARLTON ↓

Pockley Moor

Birk Nab is a classic example of a Tabular Hill. Rising to 1015 feet, it is well seen from north of the farm. Some distance to left and right are its neighbours Boon Hill and Roppa Edge respectively.

'Hanging Stone named on OS map, but not visible.

②

9

9

Birk Nab

9

St. Mary Magdalen, East Moors

Birk Nab Farm

POCKLEY →

①

Bonfield Gill

At the outset of the walk Birk Nab dominates a scene of all-round loveliness, with bracken, pastures and woods descending in stages to the beck.

East Moors Wood

COCKAYNE ↑

N

Lund Farm

Eastmoors Church

CARLTON 2½ miles ↓

The tiny church of St. Mary Magdalen was built in 1882 to serve the scattered communities of East Moors. It is now within the parish of Pockley. Almost hidden in trees, its other protection is its lack of windows on its north side.

WALK 8

4½ miles

THE FORGE VALLEY
from Ayton

An easy walk through glorious woodland

looking
north-west

Forge Valley

Ayton
Castle   R.Derwent

Osborne Lodge

West
Ayton ←

East
Ayton

Park by the hotel or the river in West Ayton. Alternative start: one of the two car-parks by the roadside along the Forge Valley.

THE WALK

From the road bridge separating the villages turn towards East Ayton, leaving the main road just after the post office along Castlegate. The road soon leaves the village and drops down to the River Derwent, being followed until our route takes a steep path up through the trees at the second footpath sign on the right, a little beyond a weir. At the top the path turns left to run along the top of the wood to Osborne Lodge Farm. Just after it the path drops down and merges with another, then running along to the right soon emerges onto a road.

Turn left to a junction and then left again. On approaching the second of two car parks, a path descends to a wooden footbridge over the river from where a footpath heads downstream clinging to the waters edge. At a second stile the river is forsaken as the path runs below the woods, rising to a gate to pass beneath Ayton Castle. Just beyond a short street is entered. Turn left at the end then left again on Mill Lane, to rejoin the main road in the company of the Derwent once more.

Ayton Castle

32

The Forge Valley is the name given to a two-mile length of the river Derwent as it forces its way south through a narrow break in the Tabular Hills to effect its escape into the Vale of Pickering. So named because an iron foundry – possibly established by the monks of Rievaulx – existed here until the late 18th century, the valley is a scene of wooded beauty in a corner of the Park known more for its dull blankets of conifers. Of sufficient importance to be a National Nature Reserve, the valley bottom is filled by the untainted river and parallel road, and all else is slopes dominated by ash, oak and the like – a living relic from ancient times. Enjoy this one alone!

Returning to the Derwent, a glance at the 1" Tourist map will show that logic dictates the river should flow east into the sea. This situation was remedied by Sir George Cayley of nearby Brompton in the early 19th century, who undid the work of the Ice Age by cutting a channel to link the Derwent with the North Sea at Scalby Mills. It does however only divert excess water in order to prevent flooding, and the Derwent still flows a few dozen miles more to join the Ouse near Selby.

Ayton Castle displays itself well across the river as we leave East Ayton, but our route runs right by it at the end of the walk; the ruins can be viewed from the outside only. It was built by the Evers family in the 14th century as a pele tower (i.e. fortified house) and commands a wide view over the Vale of Pickering to the Wolds. Alongside is an extensive network of earthworks.

The twin villages of East and West Ayton are linked by a long, graceful bridge, upstream of which, at the end of our walk, is a converted three-storey mill in a pleasant setting. In East Ayton, meanwhile, the church dates in part from the 13th century.

There are some spectacular glimpses across the valley and further up the Derwent.

Osborne Lodge (farm)

From the wall-side look back to see the level plain backed by the long line of the Wolds.

HACKNESS

SCARBOROUGH

River Derwent

Forge Valley

weir

N

Ayton Castle

hotel

East Ayton

West Ayton

PICKERING A170

SCARBOROUGH A170

River Derwent

WALK 9

5 miles

LEVISHAM MOOR AND NEWTON DALE

From Levisham

A highly scenic exploration of the environs of Levisham

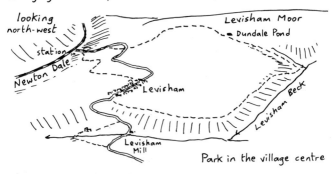

Park in the village centre

THE WALK

Leave the village by the road to Lockton, but as it leaves the houses to drop through the woods take a narrow path heading away from the seat on the left. It remains a narrow but clear path as it undulates along the top of the steep bracken slope: at an early stage be sure to fork left to remain at the top, for a more inviting arm descends towards the beck below. At a sharp corner our upper path swings left to run along Levisham Brow, dropping a little before a fuller descent to an intervening gate. Just a little further on is a guidepost by the beck: here turn sharp left to follow a wide track up the side of Dundale Griff.

At the moor top take the narrower right fork which runs gently along to Dundale Pond. From the junction of paths here either continue on past the pond to a wall-corner, or (for better views) take the path rising half-left to a wall, and then turn right to the wall-corner. Now follow this wall away to its next corner, then leave it by tracing a prominent mound to the edge of a steep drop. A path then descends to the road to Levisham station, cutting a corner of the sharp bend and rejoining the road to reach the station at the bottom of the hill.

Our return path starts at a gate into the woods

just above the station (on the right, climbing back up), from where a path rises through the trees to emerge into a field. At the top a stile gives access to a track which forks just to the right. Take the path rising uniformly to arrive at a seat, there taking the right-hand path at another fork. This path contours round the head of Keldgate Slack to a gate at the far end. From it take a stile on the left to rise by a field-edge before joining a back lane to re-enter Levisham.

Levisham has as many man-made features of interest out of the village as within it. The walk already takes in the railway station in Newton Dale, but Levisham's own lesser valley also has much to offer. The first item is the church of St. Mary, a former parish church which dates from the 11th century but was made new as recently as the 19th. Today it is but a shell, being steadily engulfed by undergrowth – maybe one day it will be restored again. It can be seen from the main path after leaving Levisham.

Only 350 yards further upstream is another building which has lost its true vocation, for there are now holiday cottages at the former mill. It remains, however, a highly attractive scene, with ducks splashing by the beck, and a rusting waterwheel in situ. The extended map shows a worthwhile extension to include all this.

St. Mary's, Levisham

Levisham railway station stands a good two miles from the village by road, though Newton-on-Rawcliffe, the line's nearest village, is only a half-mile distant on foot. In its isolated position on the floor of Newton Dale, it is one of only two stations on the 18 mile line between Grosmont and Pickering. Closed by British Railways in 1965, the line was rescued from oblivion by enthusiasts to create the North Yorkshire Moors Railway. The sight of steam on this impressive route is a marvellous spectacle, and one that, with luck, can be enjoyed on reaching the moor-edge at its highest point. Below is the deep trough of Newton Dale with its well wooded slopes (see also Walk 2) and the road down to the station highly prominent.

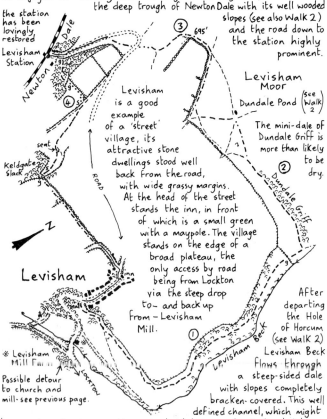

the station has been lovingly restored

Levisham Station

Newton Dale

695'

Levisham Moor

Dundale Pond (see Walk 2)

The mini-dale of Dundale Griff is more than likely to be dry.

Dundale Griff

Levisham is a good example of a 'street' village, its attractive stone dwellings stood well back from the road, with wide grassy margins. At the head of the street stands the inn, in front of which is a small green with a maypole. The village stands on the edge of a broad plateau, the only access by road being from Lockton via the steep drop to — and back up from — Levisham Mill.

seat

Keldgate Slack

ROAD

Z

Levisham

inn

Levisham Beck

After departing the Hole of Horcum (see Walk 2) Levisham Beck flows through a steep-sided dale with slopes completely bracken-covered. This well defined channel, which might

* Levisham Mill Farm

Possible detour to church and mill-see previous page.

LOCKTON

be in wild country, is in reality sandwiched between good agricultural plateaux.

WALK 10
6¾ miles

FARNDALE AND WEST GILL
from Low Mill

The famous riverside 'daffodils walk' precedes a fine upland trek with classic Farndale views.

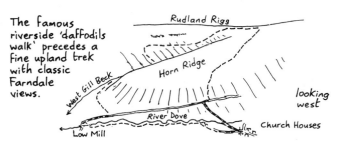

Start from the car-park at Low Mill, Farndale

THE WALK

From the car park take the adjacent gate to a footbridge over the river. The path now follows the Dove upstream, and as this forms the 'daffodil walk' (in season!) there is little chance of going astray. Numerous stiles are encountered before arrival at High Mill, a narrow lane now taking us away from the river to Church Houses.

At the first road junction turn left to re-cross the Dove before a steep climb to another junction. Here turn right only as far as the first buildings (Monket House) and then take a gate on the left. A wide track climbs the slope before easing out to cross the moor in splendid fashion. A prominent cairn on Dickon Howe is passed before reaching a crossroads with the Rudland Rigg 'road'.

Here we turn left for a little under half a mile, and just before a gentle rise bear off to the left where a beheaded 'modern' guidepost still doggedly serves its one purpose. Initially pathless, a shooters' track is very shortly joined, and is accompanied steadily down past a string of grouse butts. From the last of these a narrower path takes up a generally level course through bracken and heather.

At the top of a steepish drop through bracken – just above a wall-corner down to the left – leave the path by bearing right along the level brow of the steeper drop. At a lone and highly conspicuous little rowan a narrow path comes in from the right. Turn left along it, and a little further on, at the head of a little gill, be sure to opt for the level path left at a fork. It now runs through rampant bracken as a good green path, with the rocks of Double Crag just above us. On arriving at a rather wet area the path becomes indistinct, but by now another wall will be seen just down to the left, and the gate in it is our objective.

The moor is now vacated and a sketchy path curves down the field to a stile in the wall on the left, from where we drop down to a footbridge over West Gill Beck. Turn right to shortly rise to a barn, from where a level track heads away to Horn End Farm. Continue away on its access track to drop down to a road, with Low Mill now only five minutes along to the right.

The old road along Rudland Rigg is a splendid walkers highway, and was once a major route between the communities north and south of the moorland barrier. Whilst on it our views are largely confined to the parallel ridges of Bilsdale Moors to the right and Blakey Ridge to the left. Ahead is a whole array of Tabular Hills.

• Dickon Howe

1210'   summit of walk

Rudland Rigg

③

grouse butts

④

West Gill Head

For a while the Lion Inn at Blakey hugs the skyline eastward.

West Gill Beck

grouse butts

⑤

Double Crag

High Mill, Farndale

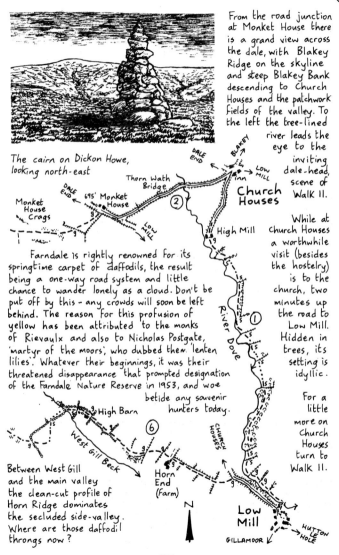

From the road junction at Monket House there is a grand view across the dale, with Blakey Ridge on the skyline and steep Blakey Bank descending to Church Houses and the patchwork fields of the valley. To the left the tree-lined river leads the eye to the inviting dale-head, scene of Walk 11.

The cairn on Dickon Howe, looking north-east

Monket House Crags

695' Monket House

Thorn Wath Bridge

DALE END

DALE END

LOW MILL

BLAKEY

LOW MILL

Church Houses

High Mill

River Dove

Farndale is rightly renowned for its springtime carpet of daffodils, the result being a one-way road system and little chance to wander lonely as a cloud. Don't be put off by this – any crowds will soon be left behind. The reason for this profusion of yellow has been attributed to the monks of Rievaulx and also to Nicholas Postgate, 'martyr of the moors', who dubbed them 'lenten lilies'. Whatever their beginnings, it was their threatened disappearance that prompted designation of the Farndale Nature Reserve in 1953, and woe betide any souvenir hunters today.

While at Church Houses a worthwhile visit (besides the hostelry) is to the church, two minutes up the road to Low Mill. Hidden in trees, its setting is idyllic.

For a little more on Church Houses turn to Walk 11.

High Barn

West Gill Beck

CHURCH HOUSES

Horn End (Farm)

Low Mill

HUTTON LE HOLE

GILLAMOOR

N

Between West Gill and the main valley the clean-cut profile of Horn Ridge dominates the secluded side-valley. Where are those daffodil throngs now?

39

WALK 11
5¾ miles

THE HEAD OF FARNDALE
from Church Houses

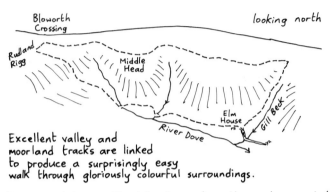

Bloworth Crossing

looking north

Rudland Rigg

Middle Head

Elm House

River Dove

Gill Beck

Excellent valley and
moorland tracks are linked
to produce a surprisingly easy
walk through gloriously colourful surroundings.

From Church Houses, Farndale, drive along the road signposted
'Dale End (East)' for 2½ miles, and park on the verge after
crossing Gill Beck. Apart from the mileage it is easily found as
just up the hill beyond, at Elm House Farm (the last up the dale),
the surfaced road ends. There is ample turning space here.

THE WALK

From Gill Beck follow the road uphill to its demise
at Elm House Farm and continue between the buildings on
the farm track which takes over. It continues a level green
way before dropping to cross a beck, rising steeply and less
clearly up the other side to a ruinous farm. Now a narrow
path continues behind the ruin to run through thick bracken.
At a gatepost (with benchmark) the path escapes the bracken
to descend to a footbridge across the infant river Dove.

A sketchy path heads along the opposite bank
of the river through rather damp terrain to two forlorn
gateposts. Continue beyond them to soon rise towards a
prominent gateway in a wall, from where a path rises onto
the open moor. Soon it forks: take the sketchy path directly
up, soon trending right to the top of a beck and then on
through the heather towards a row of grouse butts.

As the path fades pick up a landrover track midway
along the butts: when it swings left before the final one go

straight on to join the Rudland Rigg road which is just a few yards away. Turn right along this broad track to very soon arrive at Bloworth Crossing. Here the track bed of the old railway is encountered and followed to the right for two and a half straightforward miles around the headwaters of the river Dove.

Just beyond a gate (to prevent unauthorised use by vehicles) is a small embankment: between these 2 features we leave the track by descending to the highly prominent wooded head of Gill Beck directly below. Though pathless, a way can be found which is mostly on grass. On reaching the trees they will be found to hide the beginning of a deep ravine with a fine waterfall pouring over the edge.

A good path now materialises to run above the trees on the right side, descending to depart the moor at a gate. A sunken track drops down through the fields to a briefly enclosed way, which emerges almost immediately onto the road end at Elm House, only yards above our start point.

The waterfall,
Gill Beck

Elm House,
looking down Farndale

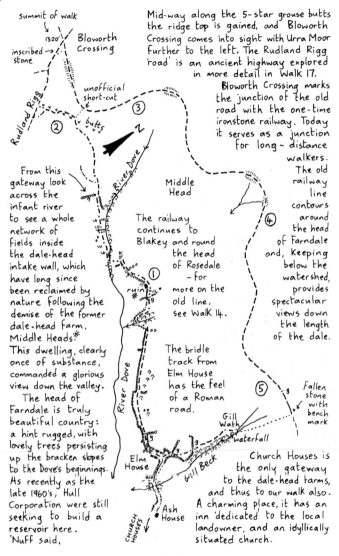

summit of walk

1320'

Bloworth Crossing

inscribed stone →

Rudland Rigg

unofficial short-cut

② ③ butts

N

Mid-way along the 5-star grouse butts the ridge top is gained, and Bloworth Crossing comes into sight with Urra Moor further to the left. The Rudland Rigg 'road' is an ancient highway explored in more detail in Walk 17.

Bloworth Crossing marks the junction of the old road with the one-time ironstone railway. Today it serves as a junction for long-distance walkers. The old railway line contours around the head of Farndale and, keeping below the watershed, provides spectacular views down the length of the dale.

From this gateway look across the infant river to see a whole network of fields inside the dale-head intake wall, which have long since been reclaimed by nature following the demise of the former dale-head farm, Middle Heads. This dwelling, clearly once of substance, commanded a glorious view down the valley.

The head of Farndale is truly beautiful country: a hint rugged, with lovely trees persisting up the bracken slopes to the Dove's beginnings. As recently as the late 1960's, Hull Corporation were still seeking to build a reservoir here. 'Nuff said.

River Dove

Middle Head

The railway continues to Blakey and round the head of Rosedale – for more on the old line, see Walk 14.

① ruin

The bridle track from Elm House has the feel of a Roman road.

River Dove

④

⑤

Fallen stone with bench mark

Gill Wath waterfall

Elm House

Gill Beck

Ash House

CHURCH HOUSES ↓

Church Houses is the only gateway to the dale-head farms, and thus to our walk also. A charming place, it has an inn 'dedicated to the local landowner, and an idyllically situated church.

42

WALK 12
8 miles

from Lastingham

A first-class moorland ramble over two broad high ridges. This should clear the lungs!

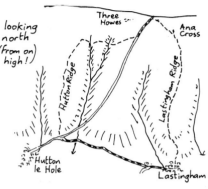

looking north (from on high!)

Park in the village centre. Alternative starts: Hutton-le-Hole (village car-park, just off-route) or alongside the open road between the villages.

| THE WALK |

     Leave the village centre by the Hutton-le-Hole road between the church and the inn. With its good proportion of grass verges this undulating road is accompanied for 1½ miles, almost as far as a junction with the moor road from Rosedale Abbey. With the guidepost in sight turn right up a green track through the bracken, crossing straight over the incoming road and up a wide track 'to Spaunton Lodge only'.

     This gently rising access track is followed for almost a mile until where it bears left and descends a little, take a green path continuing our more direct journey up the broad ridge. The path improves in quality as it maintains the steady rise to arrive at a T-junction. Here turn right on a shooters' track which is accompanied as far as a sheepfold at the 2nd of two becks encountered. Now cross the beck by the fold and rise half-left up the slope, passing a stake and easing out to preferably locate a track which materialises to lead back onto the Rosedale road. As long as there isn't too much of a trend to the left then the road will still be met at near enough the right place.

     On gaining the road turn left up it to the brow of

the hill (excellent verge again). At this point turn right on a wide path along the moor top to the beckoning Ana Cross on the skyline: a narrow path leaves the main one to gain the cross. From it a clear, cairned path continues due south, merging into a wide track to maintain the long and very gradual return to Lastingham.

At the moor edge above the village the track becomes enclosed to descend as a lane into the centre of the village.

③

Hutton Ridge

Z

625'

② HUTTON
HOLE

ROSEDALE
ABBEY

Lastingham is a delightful village sharing an identical situation as its near-neighbour Hutton-le-Hole: it shelters beneath wooded Tabular Hills while looking north to the moors. Here, however, the similarity ends. Firstly, Lastingham's houses do not stand quietly back, but huddle round a compact centre with lanes branching off in all directions. The second and more notable difference is that instead of prettiness, Lastingham's pilgrim comes seeking a shrine, that of St. Cedd.

Cedd was a Lindisfarne monk who came and founded a monastery in 654, a task completed by his brother Chad. Destroyed by the Danes two centuries later, the site of this important early Christian centre became a place of pilgrimage. In 1078 Stephen of Whitby built a crypt, and still intact beneath the present church, it is a unique Norman relic, and can be inspected.

Several wells, including one to Cedd, can be found about the village.

⑦

As the track rises above the moor road, far-reaching views of the Tabular Hills open up to the west. Sharp eyes will be able to pick out Ana Cross high on the skyline ahead and to the right.

①

High Cross

SPAUNTON

Lastingham

APPLETON-
LE-MOORS

CROPTON

inn

Lastingham Knoll

x605'

Here the environs of Lastingham finally appear, with the village all but hidden in beautiful trees.

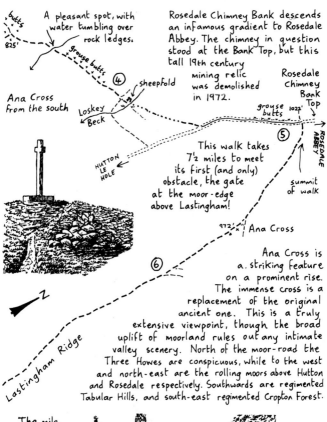

butts
825'

A pleasant spot, with water tumbling over rock ledges.

grouse butts

④ → sheepfold

Ana Cross from the south

Loskey Beck

grouse butts

HUTTON LE HOLE

Rosedale Chimney Bank descends an infamous gradient to Rosedale Abbey. The chimney in question stood at the Bank Top, but this tall 19th century mining relic was demolished in 1972.

Rosedale Chimney Bank Top

1022'

⑤

ROSEDALE ABBEY

This walk takes 7½ miles to meet its first (and only) obstacle, the gate at the moor-edge above Lastingham!

summit of walk

972' ✕ Ana Cross

⑥

Ana Cross is a striking feature on a prominent rise. The immense cross is a replacement of the original ancient one. This is a truly extensive viewpoint, though the broad uplift of moorland rules out any intimate valley scenery. North of the moor-road the Three Howes are conspicuous, while to the west and north-east are the rolling moors above Hutton and Rosedale respectively. Southwards are regimented Tabular Hills, and south-east regimented Cropton Forest.

Lastingham Ridge

The mile after Bank Top, although a well-used path, is not a right-of-way.

Lastingham

WALK 13
5¾ miles

ALONG ROPPA EDGE
from Newgate Bank

looking south-east

Roppa Edge — Rievaulx Moor — Newgate Bank — R. Seph

A very straightforward
walk making use of two parallel
tracks. Extensive views over Bilsdale,
few gradients, and few chances to go astray.

Park in the Forestry Commission car park at the top of
Newgate Bank on the B1257 five miles north of Helmsley.

THE WALK

From the main car park return almost to the road,
then take a stile on the left to follow a wide track through
the trees. On emerging it continues by a fence, endlessly yet
imperceptibly rising over Rievaulx Moor to eventually arrive at
the Ordnance column atop Roppa Edge. Just beyond it the
track meets a narrow lane: go left down it to its demise at
a crossroads of forest tracks.

Head along the track to the left – it soon escapes
from confinement to run along the foot of Roppa Edge. With
plantations returning first on the left and then completely, the
track finally joins the B1257 part-way
up Newgate Bank. Turn up as far as
an old quarry, then locate a narrow
path rising above the road to reach
an observation platform just above.
The car park is in the trees behind.

*Looking up Bilsdale
from Roppa Edge*

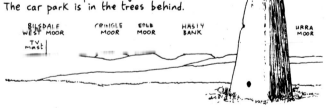

BILSDALE WEST MOOR   CRINGLE MOOR   COLD MOOR   HASTY BANK   URRA MOOR

TV mast

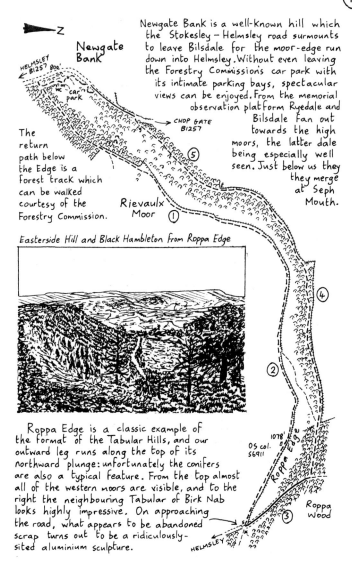

→ N

Newgate Bank

← HELMSLEY B1257 800'

WC • car park

Newgate Bank is a well-known hill which the Stokesley – Helmsley road surmounts to leave Bilsdale for the moor-edge run down into Helmsley. Without even leaving the Forestry Commission's car park with its intimate parking bays, spectacular views can be enjoyed. From the memorial observation platform Ryedale and Bilsdale fan out towards the high moors, the latter dale being especially well seen. Just below us they merge at Seph Mouth.

→ CHOP GATE B1257

The return path below the Edge is a forest track which can be walked courtesy of the Forestry Commission.

⑤

Rievaulx Moor ①

Easterside Hill and Black Hambleton from Roppa Edge

④

②

1078'
OS col.
S6911

Roppa Edge

Roppa Edge is a classic example of the format of the Tabular Hills, and our outward leg runs along the top of its northward plunge: unfortunately the conifers are also a typical feature. From the top almost all of the western moors are visible, and to the right the neighbouring Tabular of Birk Nab looks highly impressive. On approaching the road, what appears to be abandoned scrap turns out to be a ridiculously-sited aluminium sculpture.

Roppa Wood

③

← HELMSLEY

WALK 14

5¼ miles

THE HEAD OF ROSEDALE

from Blakey

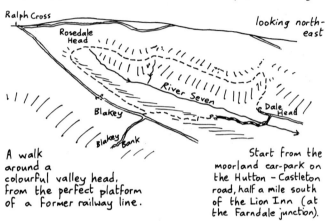

A walk
around a
colourful valley head,
from the perfect platform
of a former railway line.

Start from the
moorland car-park on
the Hutton – Castleton
road, half a mile south
of the Lion Inn (at
the Farndale junction).

THE WALK

From the car park follow the footpath sign for
Rosedale and immediately the old railway track is met.
For now though go only a yard or two to the right and
then head down the slope on a sketchy path. Soon a
wide track is met, and this takes us more gently down
to Moorlands Farm. Leave by the surfaced access road to
drop down to cross the infant river Seven, then rise up
to a T-junction. Take the road left to its demise at
Dale Head Farm.

Just level with the house use a gate on the right
('Bridleway to Great Fryup Dale') to pass around the right of
a huge barn, from where a path rises with a fence above
the beck. Higher up it trends right to a gate onto the open
moor, and a little further up through the bracken the
old railway is encountered again.

This time we are to become well acquainted, for
it is now accompanied to the left all the way round the
dale head and back to the start point. In several instances
where the line has become reed-choked, the path escapes
to take an easier parallel course.

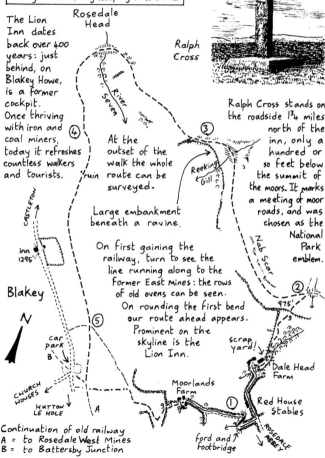

IMPORTANT : Please note the entire length of the old railway on this walk is not a public right-of-way. It can be used by courtesy of the landowners, who have the right to rescind their geniality: let's keep in the good books by keeping to the line.

Ralph Cross

The Lion Inn dates back over 400 years: just behind, on Blakey Howe, is a former cockpit. Once thriving with iron and coal miners, today it refreshes countless walkers and tourists.

Rosedale Head

River Seven

Ralph Cross stands on the roadside 1¾ miles north of the inn, only a hundred or so feet below the summit of the moors. It marks a meeting of moor roads, and was chosen as the National Park emblem.

④

③

Reeking Gill

At the outset of the walk the whole route can be surveyed.

ruin

Large embankment beneath a ravine.

On first gaining the railway, turn to see the line running along to the former East mines: the rows of old ovens can be seen.

On rounding the first bend our route ahead appears. Prominent on the skyline is the Lion Inn.

Nab Scar

②

975

CASTLETON

inn 1295'

Blakey

N

⑤

car park B

CHURCH HOUSES

HUTTON LE HOLE

A

scrap yard!

Dale Head Farm

Moorlands Farm

①

Red House Stables

ROSEDALE ABBEY

ford and footbridge

Continuation of old railway
A = to Rosedale West Mines
B = to Battersby Junction

49

The old railside ruin, looking across Rosedale Head

The Rosedale Ironstone Railway was constructed in 1861 to carry vast amounts of iron ore from the Rosedale mines to the furnaces on Teesside. One cannot fail to be impressed by this achievement of engineering: running across the moors 1000 feet up, the single line climbed from the valley by way of a steep incline then contoured around the head of Farndale to Blakey, where our walk begins. The car park stands on Blakey Ridge's narrowest point, and a junction developed here in 1865 when the line to the mines on the west side of Rosedale was joined by the line we are returning on, round the dalehead to the East Mines. The railway closed in 1929 after the demise of the mining industry, but both have left their mark. Today it is difficult to visualise a scene of thousands labouring – and living – hard in this now tranquil dale.

The Lion Inn and Blakey Howe

WALK 15

4¼ miles

| NEWGATE BROW AND MALO CROSS |

from Saltergate

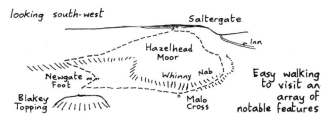

looking south-west

Saltergate

Hazelhead Moor

Newgate Foot

Whinny Nab

Blakey Topping

Malo Cross

Easy walking to visit an array of notable features

Start from the large car-park above Saltergate Bank, on the A169 half a mile south of the inn.

| THE WALK |

Before commencing the walk in earnest - or on concluding it - be sure to cross the road to witness the dramatic view down into the Hole of Horcum (scene of Walk 2).

From the car-park turn north along the road, just as far as a road to the right. This is the access road to the farm at Newgate Foot, and is pleasantly followed until it begins a steep descent thereto. Here head straight on along a wide track passing through a gate and continuing above the bank. At a forlorn gatepost opposite a stile leave the track by dropping left to a stile from where a path doubles back, to drop through the bracken slopes of Newgate Brow to a stile at the bottom. Now simply accompany the fence left to Newgate Foot Farm, two gates giving access to the main track.

Turn down the track between the buildings to a stile on the left. From the stile head across the field to a stile by a gate, from where an old track runs outside the forest fence. Part way along this gentle rise it turns sharply up the field before resuming its original course. At a gate the bracken beneath Hazelhead Moor is entered to soon arrive at Malo Cross. Here take the path left alongside the fence beneath Whinny Nab. Soon it rises to a track on the moor, running above Saltergate Brow to eventually arrive at a wood. Here the right-of-way fights its way across the tree-bound pasture in front in order to rejoin the main road, but most walkers will remain on the track which swings left, keeping outside the trees to regain the outward farm road, retracing those early steps to conclude the walk.

Malo Cross and
Whinny Nab

Blakey Topping
from Newgate Foot

Saltergate and Levisham Moor from Double Dyke

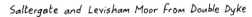

52

Saltergate's name, not surprisingly, relates to it being astride an old salt traders' route. The inn achieved a certain prominence due to its permanently burning peat fire.

Malo Cross stands at the foot of shapely Whinny Nab, a hill which it originally graced prior to being restored to its present site in modern times. It was a landmark on the old Whitby to Pickering road, and its prominent inscription is thought to refer to Richard Egerton, Knight.

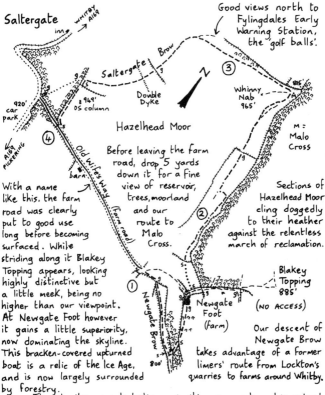

Saltergate

inn — WHITBY A169

Good views north to Fylingdales Early Warning Station, the 'golf balls'.

Saltergate Brow

Double Dyke

Whinny Nab 965'

815

③

920' car park

949' OS column

M = Malo Cross

via A169 PICKERING

④

barn

Old Wifes Way (farm road)

Hazelhead Moor

Before leaving the farm road, drop 5 yards down it for a fine view of reservoir, trees, moorland and our route to Malo Cross.

②

Sections of Hazelhead Moor cling doggedly to their heather against the relentless march of reclamation.

With a name like this, the farm road was clearly put to good use long before becoming surfaced. While striding along it Blakey Topping appears, looking highly distinctive but a little meek, being no higher than our viewpoint. At Newgate Foot however it gains a little superiority, now dominating the skyline. This bracken-covered upturned boat is a relic of the Ice Age, and is now largely surrounded by forestry.

①

Newgate Brow

Newgate Foot (farm)

Blakey Topping 885'

(NO ACCESS)

800'

Our descent of Newgate Brow takes advantage of a former limers' route from Lockton's quarries to farms around Whitby.

Though its ascent looks an inviting prospect, and is indeed an obvious one from Newgate Foot, there is no definitive right-of-way, and its owners the National Trust have no access arrangements.

WALK 16

5¼ miles

LANGDALE RIGG AND THE DERWENT

from Langdale End

Riverbank and forest walking with
a nice open-air finish

looking west

Langdale Rigg

Howden
Hill

Langdale
End

River Derwent

Park in the centre of
the hamlet, or just across the bridge over the river.

THE WALK

From the 'phone box in the centre of the hamlet
turn down the road to cross Langdale Bridge, then take a
stile on the left to follow the Derwent upstream. Guiding us
through the trees the path disappears at a gate into a long,
level pasture. At the next gate a path returns to transport
us through the forest, still with the river close by. After a
short mile cross a wooden footbridge over the Derwent to take
the path rising away.

The path climbs generally half-right with occasional
zig-zags included. On meeting a level path turn left along the
better path to soon swing up to the right again to emerge
onto a wide - and probably wet - green path. Go right along
this level way for about 500 yards until a good path heads
up to the left just short of a clearing. At an early fork the
left-hand option is best: after swinging right to rejoin the right
fork the path then rises like an incline tramway to the edge
of the forest. At a fence it turns left to a junction at the
very top of the broad ridge.

Here turn left on a path through a wide break
along the ridge top. This good level way continues for one
of those 'short' miles before escaping from the forest. Keep on
along the top of the pasture until a path materialises to
lead us down the rigg-end. At the bottom it fades, but go
half-left to a fence corner and head away with the fence to
a stile in the next corner. Once over it follow the field-edge to
drop down to a surfaced farm road. Go left along it to join a
road and then left again to soon return to Langdale End.

On gaining the ridge top there is a brief distant view out of the forest to moorland around the Scarborough - Whitby road to the north-east.

Our route through the forest has something of a 'Jekyll' and 'Hyde' character. At no point do we tread the usual forest road: instead a mixture of riverside paths, steep zig-zags and grassy rides. Though short sections can be wet, the vast majority are pleasant underfoot. As forest walking goes, this is good.

From the forest footbridge to the ridge top we are on the route of the Allerston-Reasty Walk, a 16 mile trek devised by the Forestry Commission. Its waymark occurs at regular intervals in the shape of a blue man striding joyfully out. This is the only part where we depart from rights-of-way for the Commission's permissive path.

Leaving the trees behind on Langdale Rigg is a good moment, eagerly anticipated, and with good views down the Derwent valley: directly ahead is the conical Howden Hill. Afforestation, however, is still the dominant feature - note the blanket draped over the steep Langdale slopes above our outward route. Note also, on our right side (west) four near-identical rounded spurs cloaked in conifers, but with green pastures still remaining slotted in between them all.

Langdale End is an isolated farming hamlet with an untouched inn. Towards the bridge is the simple church of St.Peter. Above the houses rises Howden Hill, diminutive when seen from the Rigg, but shapely and tree-free! - though sadly footpath-free also.

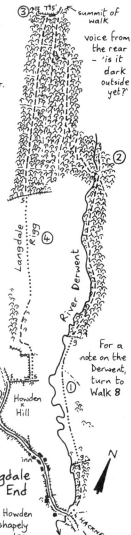

③ 915 775' summit of walk

voice from the rear - 'is it dark outside yet?'

②

Langdale Rigg ④

River Derwent

For a note on the Derwent, turn to Walk 8

①

BICKLEY

⑤ Howden × Hill

inn

Langdale End

HACKNESS

N

WALK 17
6¼ miles

BRANSDALE HEAD AND RUDLAND RIGG
from Cockayne

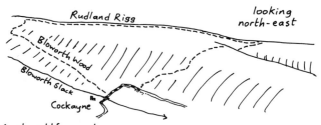

A straightforward walk on excellent tracks, with far-reaching views over Bransdale and Farndale

Cockayne stands at the head of Bransdale, 10 miles from Helmsley and Kirkbymoorside. Park on the roadside near the cattle-grid beneath the church.

THE WALK

From the cattle-grid take the Kirkbymoorside road down across the beck. At the first bend up the other side, turn left through a gate and follow a track into the large plantation of Bloworth Wood. With no other tracks to lead us astray this well-surfaced forest road rises at a gentle gradient towards the end of the plantation. At the top end of the trees the moor is reached: turn right through the gate and up the track to very quickly gain the top of Rudland Rigg.

Turn right along the splendid old road as it favours first the Bransdale and then the Farndale side of the broad ridge. This remains our course for well over two miles, until a crossroads with a track of equal stature. Turn right along it, crossing a tiny beck before descending to the road in Bransdale at Cow Sike.

Turn right to return, very shortly, to the start point.

The Cammon Stone

56

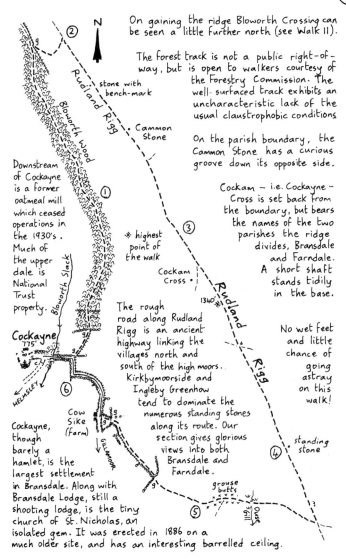

On gaining the ridge Bloworth Crossing can be seen a little further north (see Walk 11).

The forest track is not a public right-of-way, but is open to walkers courtesy of the Forestry Commission. The well-surfaced track exhibits an uncharacteristic lack of the usual claustrophobic conditions

On the parish boundary, the Cammon Stone has a curious groove down its opposite side.

Cockam — i.e. Cockayne — Cross is set back from the boundary, but bears the names of the two parishes the ridge divides, Bransdale and Farndale. A short shaft stands tidily in the base.

No wet feet and little chance of going astray on this walk!

N

Rudland Rigg

stone with bench-mark

Cammon Stone

Bloworth Wood

Downstream of Cockayne is a former oatmeal mill which ceased operations in the 1930's. Much of the upper dale is National Trust property.

Bloworth Slack

*highest point of the walk

Cockam Cross

1340 *

Rudland Rigg

Cockayne 775'

HELMSLEY

6

The rough road along Rudland Rigg is an ancient highway linking the villages north and south of the high moors.. Kirkbymoorside and Ingleby Greenhow tend to dominate the numerous standing stones along its route. Our section gives glorious views into both Bransdale and Farndale.

Cow Sike (farm)

GILLAMOOR

standing stone

4

Cockayne, though barely a hamlet, is the largest settlement in Bransdale. Along with Bransdale Lodge, still a shooting lodge, is the tiny church of St. Nicholas, an isolated gem. It was erected in 1886 on a much older site, and has an interesting barrelled ceiling.

grouse butts

5

Ouse Gill

St. Nicholas Church, Cockayne

WALK 18
6¾ miles

GILLAMOOR AND DOUTHWAITE DALE
from Hutton-le-Hole

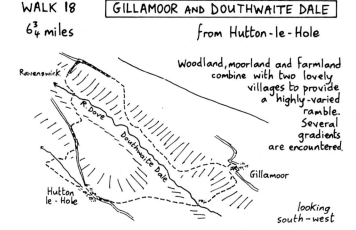

Woodland, moorland and farmland
combine with two lovely
villages to provide
a highly-varied
ramble.
Several
gradients
are encountered.

*looking
south-west*

Start from the main car-park in Hutton-le-Hole

THE WALK

From the village centre take the Castleton road out
of the north end of the village, and leave it by a stile on the
left where the parallel side road comes in (after the last house
on the left). Follow the fence right to another stile, then cross
half-left to a gate. Head along to a right-hand fence then
accompany it to a stile onto a track between hedgerows. At its
demise remain with the fence to a stile onto a bracken-cloaked
heath.

Choose the path heading half-left, avoiding a left
fork early on but then taking a lesser path right within only
another fifty yards. It briefly escapes the bracken to descend
slowly, becoming a little overgrown on returning to the bracken.
A better path soon merges from the right and runs down by
the side of a fence to join a farm track. Go right a few yards
then drop to a footbridge and into a field. Cross straight over
to a stile and across again to one in the next field corner. A
fence is then followed down to a metal footbridge across the
river Dove.

From the bridge a path runs to the former mill a
short distance ahead, passing round to the right of the building
to its access track. This is accompanied uphill until a path

goes into the trees on the left: it soon narrows and then rises unfailingly to emerge into Gillamoor village. Head along the street and left at the junction, then leave the road at the first bend by taking the lane straight on. At an early kink in it go through a gate on the left and follow the fence away, two intervening fences being easily surmounted in the absence of stiles. After the second of these head half-right to a fence-corner, and just beyond is a gate and a track down through a wood.

After a brief spell of freedom from the trees, the wood is re-entered only for the same thing to happen further on. A long sketchy section 'twixt river and forest now ensues before once again joining the trees. Cross straight over at a crossroads of wide tracks and up a steepish pull to merge into a broad track at the top. Going left along the forest top, the way becomes surfaced before a left turn to Ravenswick.

Head down between the buildings to the road-end at the riverbank. Take the left track to a footbridge over the Dove, and follow a wide track up the opposite slope. Rising through the pleasant open country of Hutton Common our way becomes surfaced before meeting the Kirkbymoorside to Hutton-le-Hole road. For a straightforward finish turn left along the road, with its large proportion of grass verges, to drop down into the village.

A rather more adventurous conclusion involves a minor assault course: if interested, leave the road at a gate set back on the right just as the road is about to commence its descent towards the red roofs of Hutton. A path heads away and turns left into a wood to drop down to a novel crossing of Hutton Beck. A steep little pull past the plantation opposite leads, by bearing left above the trees, to a gate onto a wide track. Turn left along it to soon arrive back in the village.

Gillamoor is a street village on the edge of a plateau, and is renowned for its surprise view: Farndale, Lowna and Blakey Ridge feature in a glorious vista from the environs of St. Aidan's church. Dating from 1802, its absence of windows to north and east is a sign of respect for the elements. Note also the freestanding stone sundial in the main street.

River Dove

Hutton Common

KIRKBYMOORSIDE ←

Ravenswick (Farm)

trout farm

By the old ford is a former watermill.

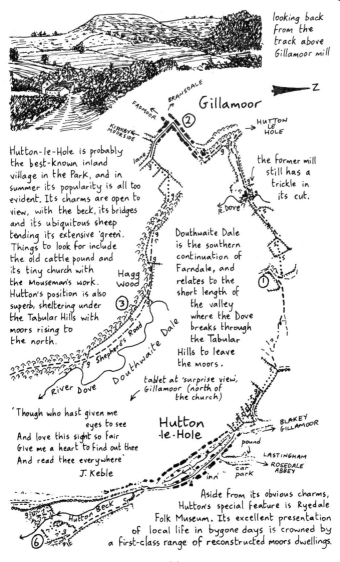

looking back
from the
track above
Gillamoor mill

Z

BRANSDALE

FADMOOR

Gillamoor

KIRKBYE
MOORSIDE

HUTTON
LE
HOLE

②

lane

the former mill
still has a
trickle in
its cut.

R. DOVE?

Hutton-le-Hole is probably
the best-known inland
village in the Park, and in
summer its popularity is all too
evident. Its charms are open to
view, with the beck, its bridges
and its ubiquitous sheep
tending its extensive 'green'.
Things to look for include
the old cattle pound and
its tiny church with
the Mouseman's work.
Hutton's position is also
superb, sheltering under
the Tabular Hills with
moors rising to
the north.

Hagg
Wood

③

Shepherd's Road

Douthwaite Dale

River Dove

Douthwaite Dale
is the southern
continuation of
Farndale, and
relates to the
short length of
the valley
where the Dove
breaks through
the Tabular
Hills to leave
the moors.

①

tablet at 'surprise view',
Gillamoor (north of
the church)

'Though who hast given me
            eyes to see
And love this sight so fair
Give me a heart to find out thee
And read thee everywhere'
            J. Keble

**Hutton
-le-Hole**

BLAKEY
GILLAMOOR

pound

LASTINGHAM

ROSEDALE
ABBEY

inn

car
park

Hutton Beck

⑥

Aside from its obvious charms,
Hutton's special feature is Ryedale
Folk Museum. Its excellent presentation
of local life in bygone days is crowned by
a first-class range of reconstructed moors dwellings.

LOG OF THE WALKS

These two pages provide an opportunity to maintain a permanent record of the walks completed

WALK	DATE	TIME Start	Finish	WEATHER	COMMENTS
1					
2					
3					
4					
5					
6					
7					
8					

WALK	DATE	TIME		WEATHER	COMMENTS	
		Start	Finish			
9						
10						
11						
12						
13						
14						
15						
16						
17						
18						

KEY TO THE MAP SYMBOLS

direction of north

scale
2½ inches = 1 mile

Route — clear — sketchy — no visible path

Route on public road — unenclosed — wall — fence/hedge

River/beck — bridge

Marsh

Peat grough

Crags

Limestone clints

Loose rocks/ scree

Cairns
summit   other

Trees

Buildings

Church

Abbreviations
c = cattle grid
s = stile
g = gate

Miles from start
③

THE COUNTRY CODE

Respect the life and work of the countryside
Protect wildlife, plants and trees
Keep to public paths across farmland
Safeguard water supplies
Go carefully on country roads
Keep dogs under control
Guard against all risks of fire
Fasten all gates
Leave no litter – take it with you
Make no unnecessary noise
Leave livestock, crops and machinery alone
Use gates and stiles to cross fences, hedges
and walls